THE DISCOVERY OF THE AMERICAS

by Betsy and Giulio Maestro

SCHOLASTIC INC.
NEW YORK TORONTO LONDON AUCKLAND SYDNEY

ISBN 0-590-46515-5

 Published by Scholastic Inc., 730 Broadway, New York, NY 10003, by arrangement with Lothrop, Lee & Shepard Books, a division of William Morrow & Company, Inc.

12 11 10 9 8 7 6 3 4 5 6 7/9

Printed in the U.S.A. 08

First Scholastic printing, September 1992

Many thousands of years ago, the world was a very different place. During the last Ice Age, a natural bridge formed between the land mass we call Asia and what is now North America.

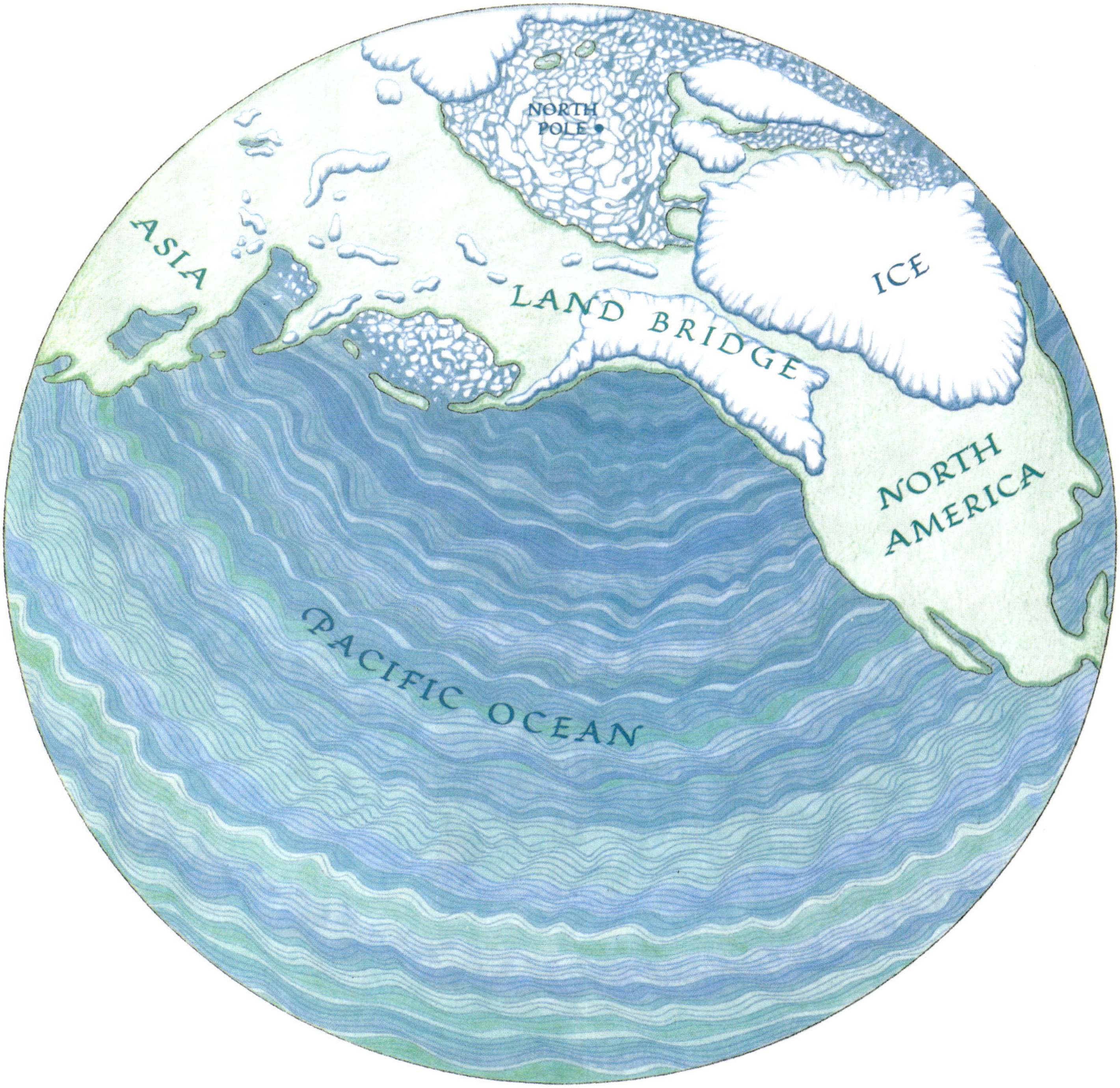

All over Asia, small groups of wandering people, or nomads, moved from place to place in search of food. They hunted large animals, including huge mastodons and mammoths, using weapons made of stone. They ate what food they could find, and when it was gone, they moved on.

Following the large game animals, these Stone Age hunters crossed over from Asia into what would later be called the New World. No one knows exactly when the first people arrived in the Americas, but it was probably at least twenty thousand years ago.

LAND BRIDGE
ICE
NORTH AMERICA
ATLANTIC
CENTRAL AMERICA
THE EQUATOR
SOUTH AMERICA
PACIFIC OCEAN

This movement, or migration, of people continued very slowly over thousands of years. New groups moved across from Asia, and earlier arrivals moved farther into the new land. Gradually people spread throughout what are now Canada, the United States, Mexico, Central and South America.

During this time, Earth's climate was changing. Temperatures slowly grew warmer, and the ice that covered much of the globe began to melt. The oceans rose, and around twelve thousand years ago the land link between Asia and North America was covered by water. No more people would come to the New World on foot.

The way people lived also began to change. The large game animals gradually died out, possibly because of the warmer temperatures or because hunters killed too many. With the large game mostly gone, the hunting nomads had to search for new kinds of food.

As people in the New World began to fish, gather fruits and nuts, and hunt smaller game, they stopped moving from place to place. They built simple homes, and small settlements grew up. After a while they began to plant and harvest their own food. Corn was one of the first crops raised by these early farmers.

Each group had its own way of life, depending on its land and climate. Some groups did continue to move around for part of the year, following the herds of buffalo.

Over a period of time, a number of great civilizations grew up in the Americas. These cultures built cities, devised written languages, and had their own religious beliefs and customs.

The Maya people, for instance, constructed about sixty cities in the area that is now Mexico and Central America. Their great temples and pyramids show that they were master builders. They were skillful in mathematics and astronomy and created a calendar that was highly accurate. Accomplished Maya artists produced pottery, sculpture, and jewelry.

During this time there was no way for new settlers or explorers to come to the Americas overland. However, it is possible that some early voyages were made by sea. As long ago as five thousand years, Japanese fishermen may have accidentally reached South America, perhaps after getting lost in a storm on the Pacific Ocean. The seafaring Phoenicians did have ships capable of long ocean voyages and may have crossed the Atlantic to trade with people in the Americas more than two thousand years ago. It is possible that, later, Chinese sailors reached the west coast of the Americas.

No one knows for sure whether any of these voyages really happened, but pottery and other objects that have been found in the Americas show amazing similarity to some found in the Old World. The answer to this puzzle is still a mystery.

Possible routes of early contacts between the Old World and the New World

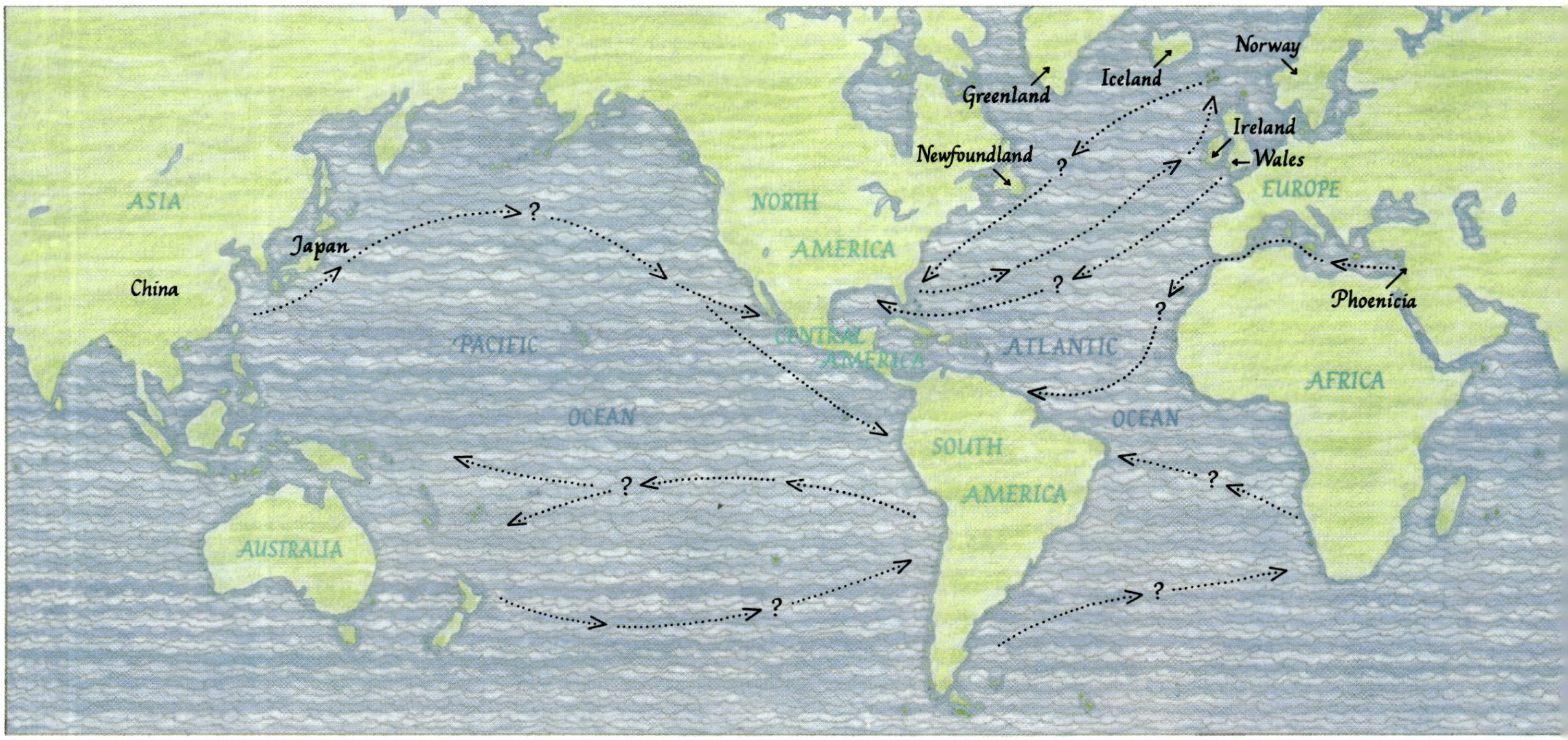

THE OLD WORLD

Pottery pieces
from Japan

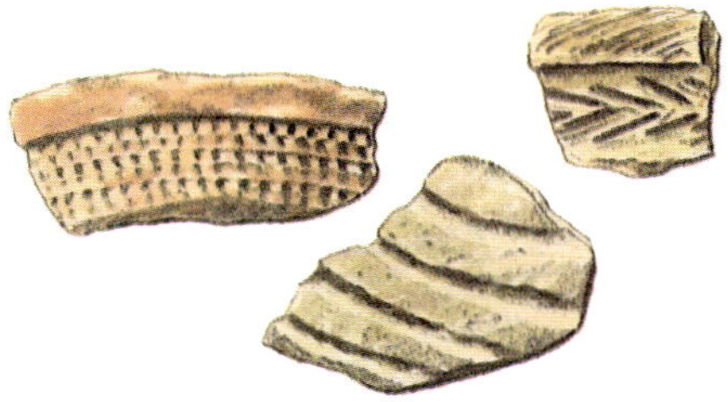

An elephant on wheels
from India

A stone fishhook
from the South Pacific

A pottery house
from Indochina

A string cross
from India

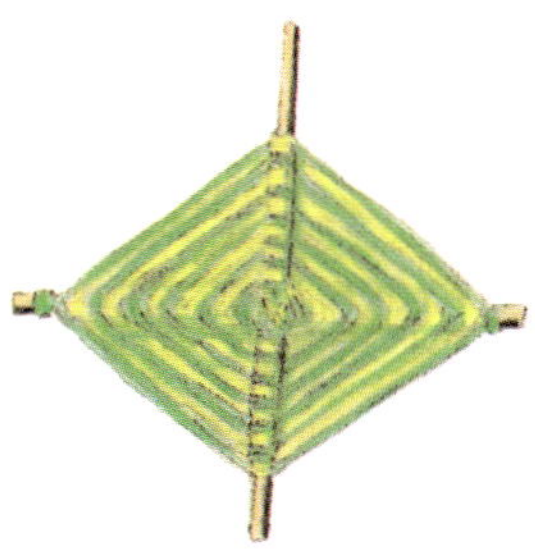

A stone carving of a Phoenician reed boat

THE NEW WORLD

Pottery pieces
from South America

A dog on wheels
from Central America

A stone fishhook from the
west coast of North America

A pottery house
from South America

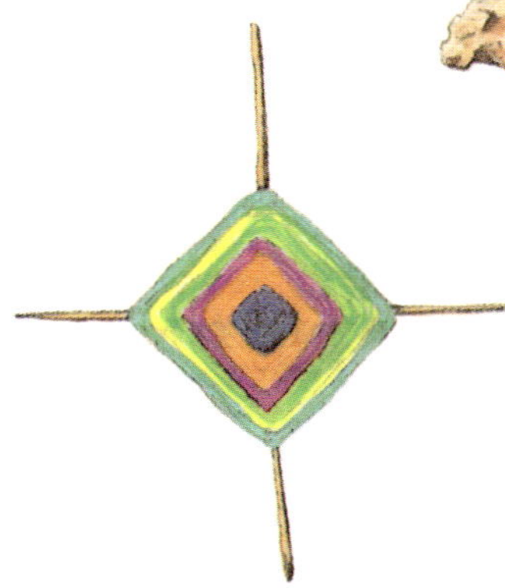

A string cross
from Central America

A South American reed boat

Saint Brendan, an Irish monk, is said to have made a voyage of discovery across the Atlantic in a small wood and leather boat during the sixth century, more than fourteen hundred years ago. Whether his journey was real or imagined is not known, but the fascinating written story of his voyage was read all over Europe and may have encouraged later explorers to seek the magical lands it described.

The first proven sea voyage to the Americas was made by the Vikings of Norway. Bjarni Herjolfsson first sighted North America in the tenth century, and Leif Ericsson actually landed there in the year 1000.

Leif Ericsson's father, Eric the Red, sailed from Norway to Iceland and then to Greenland, where he started a colony. Leif sailed from Greenland to what is now Newfoundland, an island off the coast of Canada. The Vikings called this new land Vinland, and small groups of them tried a number of times to found a permanent colony there. However, their contacts with the native people were sometimes violent, and their life was harsh and isolated. The Vikings finally gave up and left Vinland forever. The larger Viking colony in Greenland lasted for almost five hundred years before dying out.

There are many stories of Prince Madoc of Wales sailing to North America in the twelfth century, but no real traces of his visit have been found. Most people do not believe the stories of his journey to be true.

All over North and South America, the descendants of the first Americans continued to live and change. Although the Maya thrived in Mexico and Central America for thousands of years, most Native American cultures were more short-lived.

The Hopewell people, builders of mound cities in many places in North America, existed for more than six hundred years. The great Inca Empire, however, lasted for less than one hundred. The descendants of many of these groups still live in areas of the Americas today. Archeologists are still searching for and finding clues to these ancient peoples' lives buried in the earth.

For nearly five hundred years following Leif Ericsson's voyages, no new explorers seem to have come to the Americas. Few people in Europe knew about the Viking discoveries in North America. There was poor communication between distant places, and knowledge of the rest of the world was limited.

During this time, Europeans had little interest in such perilous sea voyages to faraway lands. They were too busy at home, fighting wars among themselves, battling disease, and journeying to the Middle East on religious crusades. Toward the end of this period, Marco Polo and other adventurers and traders began to travel to the Far East, bringing back silk, spices, and other exotic goods very welcome in Europe.

Marco Polo's route by land and sea

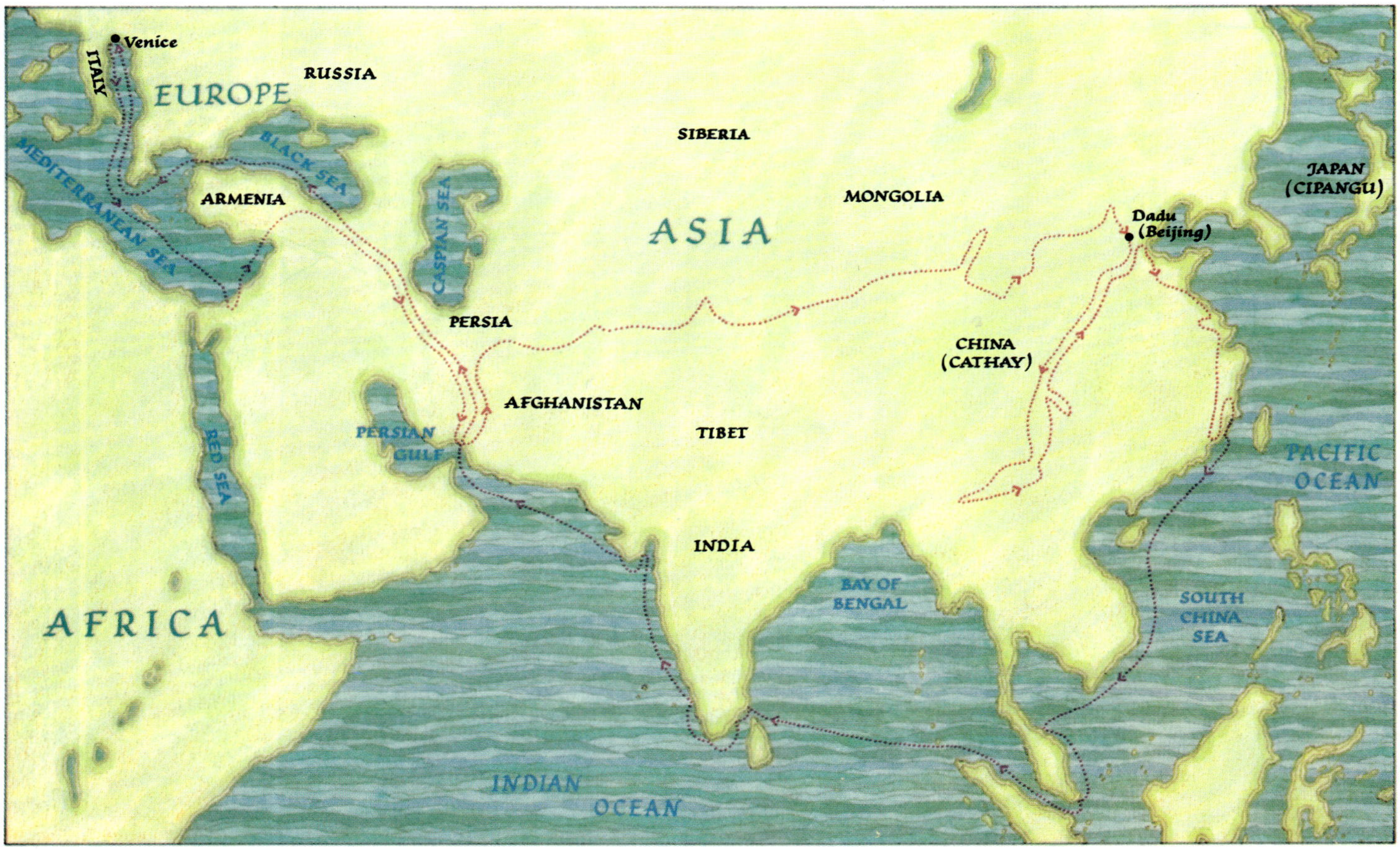

The overland trade routes to China and India were long and hard to travel. About one hundred years after these routes opened, they were closed to Europeans as a result of unrest in many areas. So Europe was forced to look for a sea route to the Far East.

This search began an exciting period in European history. It was a time of learning, growth, and discovery. Early in the fifteenth century, Portuguese explorers began making many voyages to islands in the Atlantic and along the African coast. In 1488, Bartolomeu Dias sailed down the west coast of Africa and rounded the Cape of Good Hope at the southern tip. A sea route to India now seemed possible, and some years later Vasco da Gama would reach India by continuing from where Dias had stopped.

Routes of Dias and da Gama

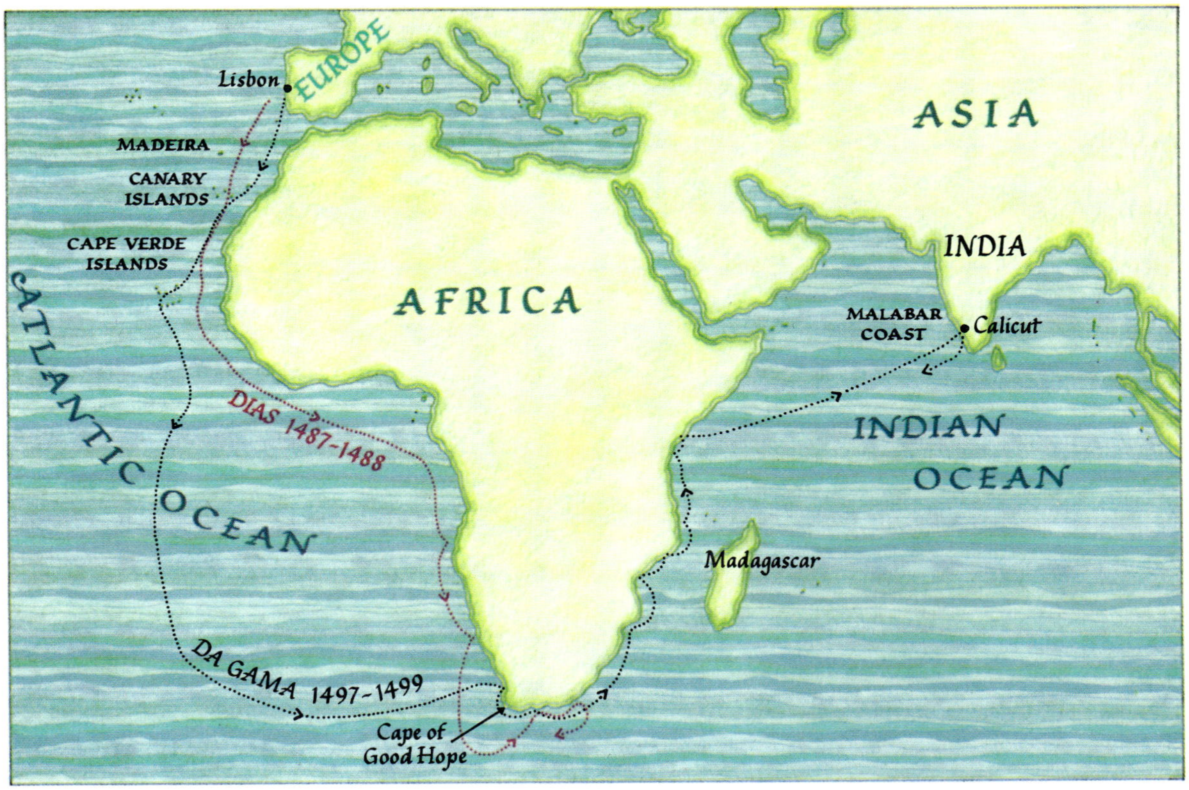

But Cristoforo Colombo, whom we know as Christopher Columbus, thought he knew a better way to get to India. Columbus, born in Italy in 1451, had been sailing all his life. By the time he was thirty, he was already an experienced seaman and navigator. Columbus believed that he could reach the Far East more quickly by sailing west across the Atlantic Ocean. Many people thought Columbus was crazy, not because they believed the earth was flat, but because they were afraid the distance was too great. There was already much evidence to show that the earth was round, but no one they knew of had ever sailed out into the Atlantic and just kept going.

This globe from 1492 shows where Columbus thought he was going

Columbus needed a lot of money to pay for ships and supplies if he was to prove that his idea was right. He went to the king of Portugal, where he was living, to ask for help. When he was refused, he left for Spain, where he hoped King Ferdinand and Queen Isabella would give him the money for the voyage. They refused at first, but Columbus did not give up easily. Finally, after eight years, they agreed to help him.

On August 3, 1492, Columbus set sail with his three ships, the *Niña,* the *Pinta,* and the *Santa María,* on his historic journey. With only a compass and the stars to help him, Columbus guided his ships across the Atlantic.

The distance was very great, and life on board ship was miserable. Columbus and his crew were all very relieved when at last they sighted land on October 12, 1492. Columbus was sure that he had reached a part of Asia, but his first landfall was actually an island in the Bahamas. He sailed on to other islands, including Cuba, which he thought might be part of China or Japan. Columbus had rediscovered the Americas, although he did not know it.

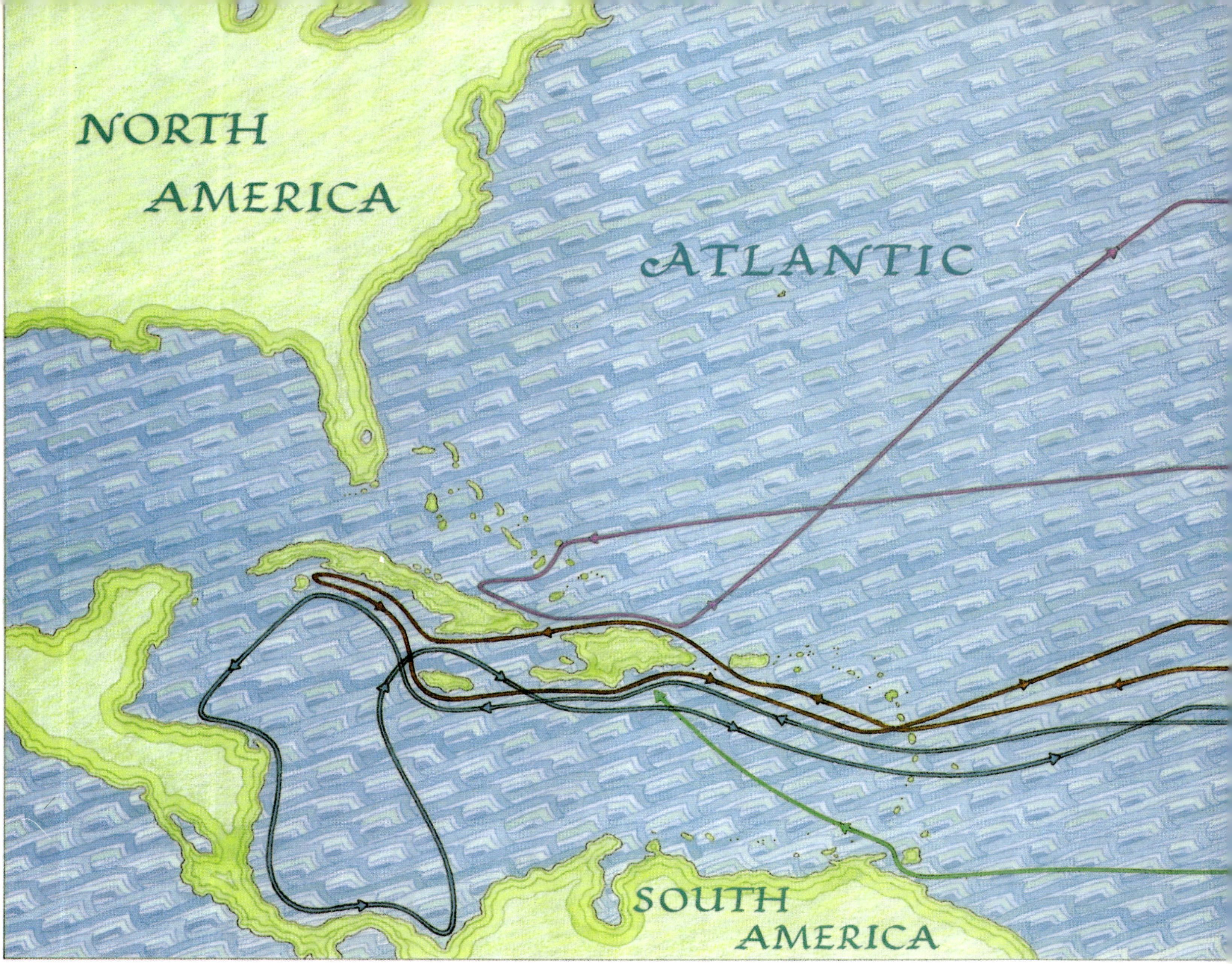

Columbus's four routes to the Americas, 1492–1504

Columbus made three more voyages to the Americas for Spain. He visited Puerto Rico, Jamaica, and Trinidad, and on his third trip he traveled along the coast of South America. Until his death in 1506, Columbus insisted that he had reached the East Indies. He believed that if he had continued on, he would have found China. Columbus was wrong. To get to China, he would have had to sail around South America and across the Pacific Ocean.

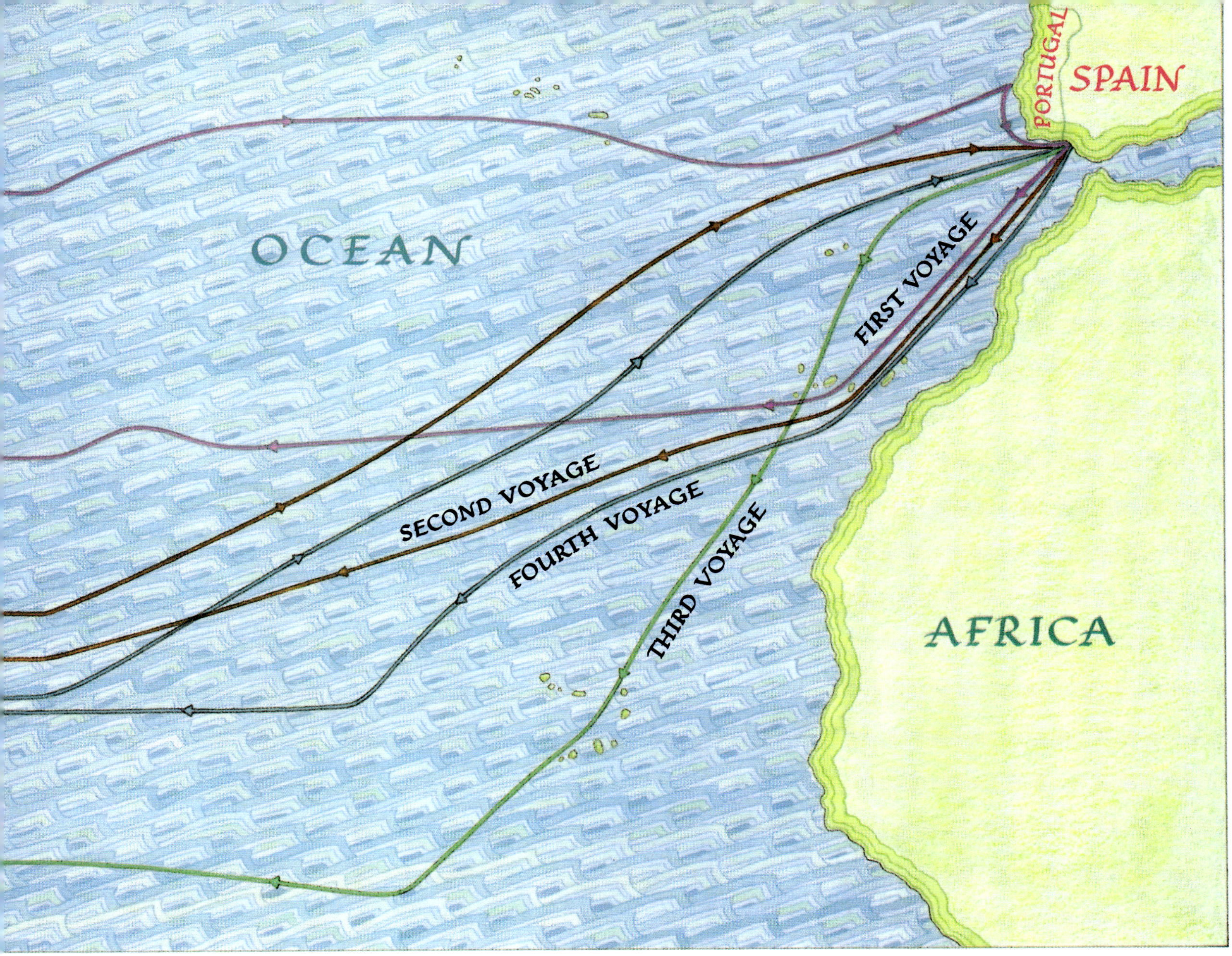

Columbus did not captain the return of the third voyage

Nevertheless, the voyages of Columbus were among the most important ever made. He discovered the best possible sea routes between Europe and the Americas, which earned him the title "The Great Navigator." He proved to all that such a long sea journey was possible, and in doing so he opened up a new world for all of Europe.

While Columbus was sailing to the Caribbean Islands and South America, another skillful Italian navigator, John Cabot, was also sent to search for a sea route to China and India. Sailing for the king of England, Cabot set out on his first journey in 1497. He took a northern route across the Atlantic and made landfall two months later in what is now Newfoundland, Canada. Five hundred years after the Vikings had landed there, John Cabot rediscovered North America.

Unfortunately, Cabot's second journey in 1498 was his last. Of his five ships, only one returned to England, and Cabot himself was never heard from again. Although very little is known about his life or his voyages, Cabot's great journeys began the English exploration and settlement of North America.

Cabot's routes to North America

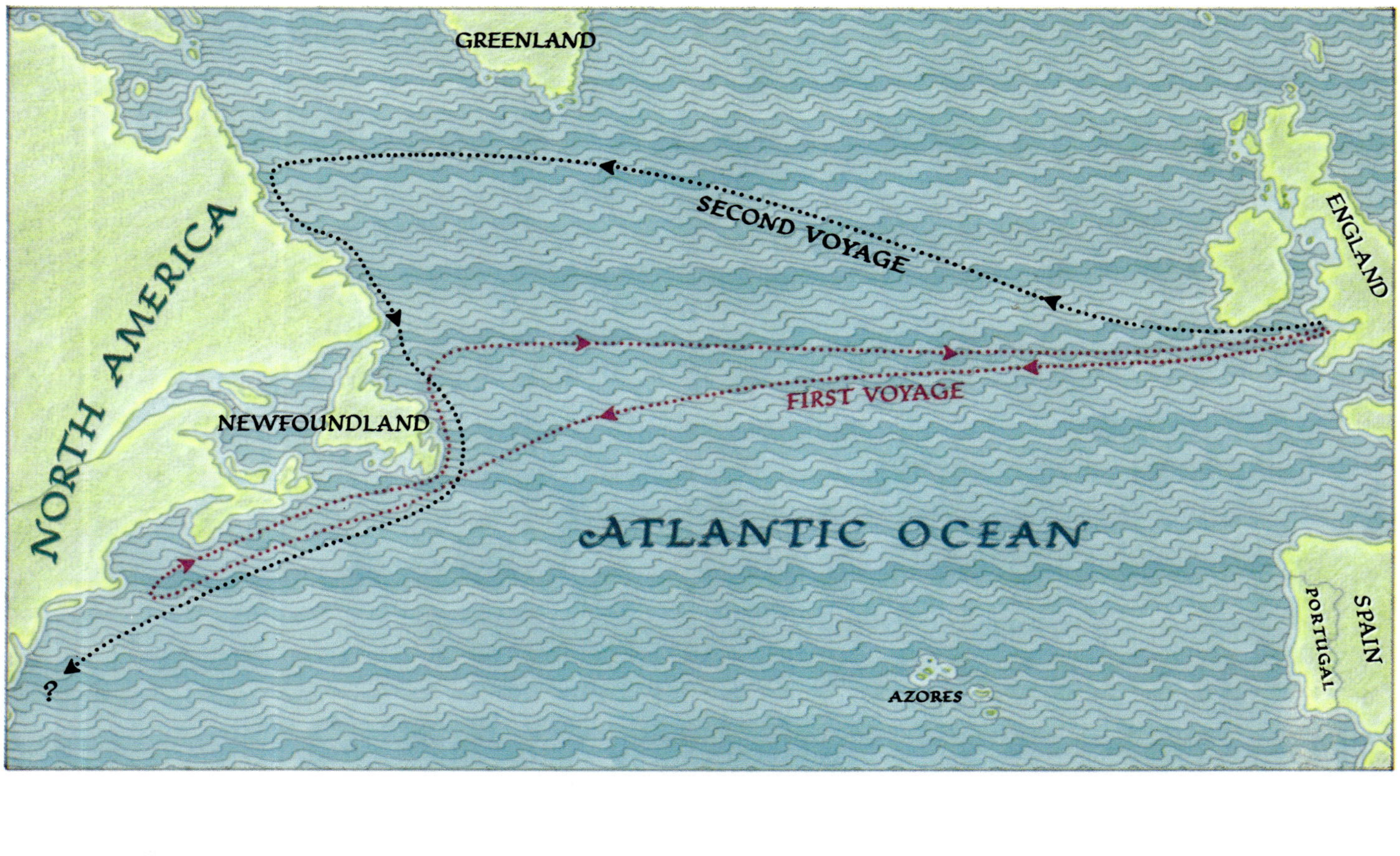

The discoveries made by Columbus and Cabot caused Europe to take a keen interest in the Americas. These unexplored lands seemed to offer the promise of vast riches, and other explorers were soon sent off across the Atlantic. One of these was Amerigo Vespucci, another Italian, who in 1499 began a number of voyages that followed the routes of Columbus.

As Vespucci traveled down the South American coast, he felt sure that the lands found by Columbus were part of another continent, not known before. Although many others shared this belief, Vespucci was the one to write about it, in an article that was published and widely read all over Europe. In 1507 a mapmaker who thought that Vespucci had actually discovered the New World used the name Amerigo to give the new continent its name—America.

Amerigo Vespucci

A few years later, a Spanish explorer, Vasco Nuñez de Balboa, sailed to Panama and journeyed overland through thick jungles and over mountains to reach the west coast of Central America. In 1513, from the top of a tall cliff, he sighted another large ocean, which he called the Southern Sea. He was the first European to sight the Pacific Ocean from the American shore.

Balboa was one of many European explorers who came to the New World to claim land, gold, and other riches for their countries. The Europeans did not care that the land and gold already belonged to other people, who were there before them. Although these explorers were brave men, they were often brutal and cruel to the native people. They tried to force them to accept the Christian religion and to adopt European customs. As a result, the natives did not trust the newcomers and often attacked them.

Ferdinand Magellan, born in Portugal, was an experienced sea captain who sailed for Spain. He was sure that he could sail west across the Atlantic to South America and find a sea passage, or opening, to the new ocean on the other side. He would then sail on across it to the Orient, load up with spices, and continue westward around Africa and back to Spain. If Magellan could do this, he would be the first to sail around the world.

On September 20, 1519, Magellan left Spain with five ships and about two hundred fifty men. The journey across the Atlantic was terrible, with huge storms at sea and angry fighting on board the ships.

Magellan and his crews traveled south along the coast of South America, looking for a passage to the great ocean seen by Balboa. At last, in October 1520, more than a year after the voyage began, a passage was found. During the long search, one ship was wrecked and another secretly headed back to Spain. It took Magellan and the remaining three ships thirty-eight days to reach the new ocean, which Magellan named the Pacific. This passage to the Pacific Ocean is now called the Strait of Magellan.

As Magellan and his men sailed out into the Pacific, they had no idea of the misfortune that lay ahead. The trip turned out to be disastrous. The distance was much greater than anyone had imagined, and their short supplies of food and water soon ran out. Many of the men died of starvation and disease. Finally, in 1521, they reached the Philippine islands, where, sadly, Magellan came to the end of his heroic journey. On April 27, 1521, he was killed in a battle between two native tribes.

One unseaworthy ship had to be destroyed, and there were now only two ships left of Magellan's original five. The *Trinidad,* unable to make the long journey home, started back to the Spanish settlement in South America. On her way, she was captured by the Portuguese and then finally wrecked in a storm. The *Victoria,* however, captained by Juan Sebastian del Cano, headed toward Spain by going west across the Indian Ocean and around Africa. Del Cano and the remaining crew were determined to complete the journey for their dead leader.

The route of Magellan's ships

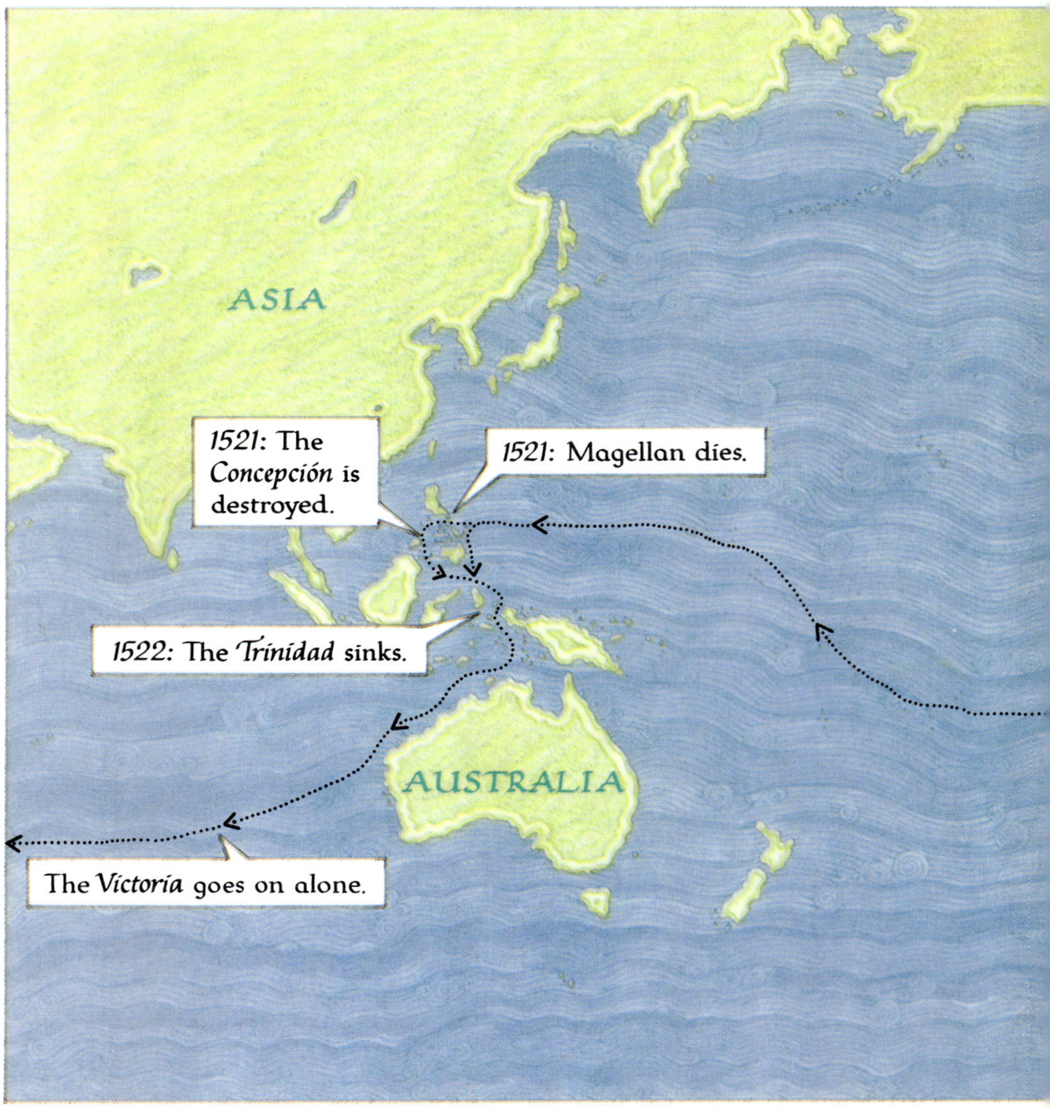

On September 8, 1522, after many more hardships and deaths, they reached Seville, Spain, exhausted but thankful to have survived. Their incredible voyage had taken almost three years, and of the two hundred fifty men who had sailed with Magellan, only eighteen returned home.

Magellan's idea had been right, and one of his ships completed the first round-the-world journey. The size of the Pacific Ocean was now known, and more accurate maps of the world could be made. At last, Europeans had a more complete view of the vast world.

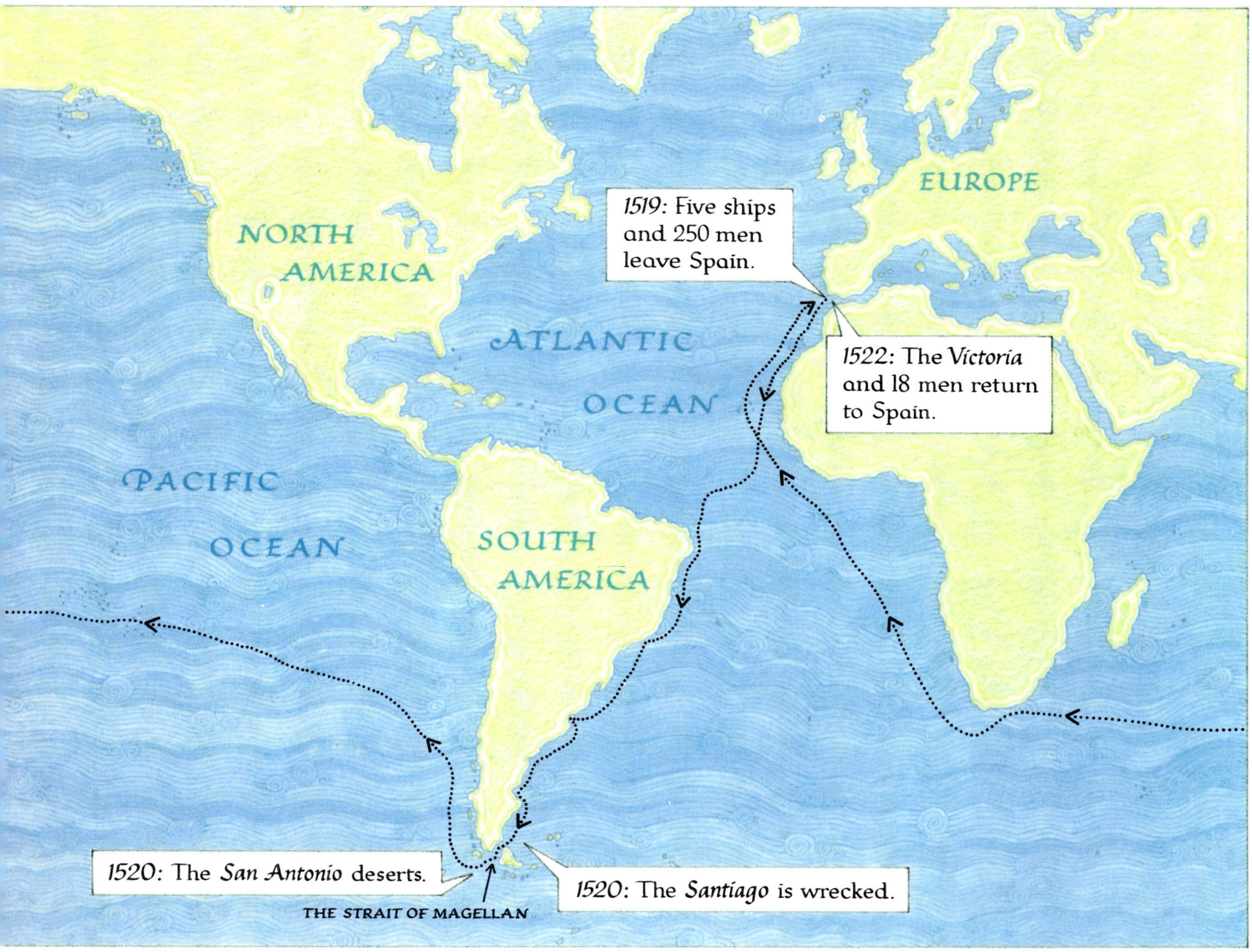

The door to the Americas was open and would never be closed again. Europe was eager to gather the riches and bounty that the New World offered.

The newcomers had knowledge, skills, and materials not yet known in the New World. Some of what the Europeans brought was good, and at first seemed wonderful and fascinating to the Native Americans. But, for them, life would never be the same.

The Europeans brought diseases that killed many of the natives, and a strange new way of life they did not understand or accept. Many lost their lives, and most lost their freedom, their customs, and their pride. They could not fight the powerful weapons the Europeans brought with them.

It was the dawn of a new time in the Americas, a time of exploration and change that would shape the future of these lands for centuries to come.

Additional Information

TABLE OF DATES

20,000 BC Arrival of first humans in North America. Estimates of arrival date vary from 60,000 to 12,000 years ago.

1500 BC Beginning of first true civilizations in the Americas.

1200 BC Rise of Phoenician sea power. Their great ships sail the Mediterranean Sea.

600 BC The Phoenicians circumnavigate Africa. Possibly, they cross the Atlantic as well.

517 BC Greek map shows the known world divided into two equal parts: Europe and Asia.

AD 120 Ptolemy, a Greek mathematician, astronomer, and geographer, constructs a series of important maps of the known world.

AD 200 Beginning of a time of high achievement among many of the civilizations in the Americas.

AD 550 Possible voyages of the Chinese and Saint Brendan to the Americas around this time.

AD 770 The Vikings discover Iceland.

AD 868 First printed book in China. Printing will not be introduced in Europe for hundreds of years.

AD 982 The Vikings discover Greenland and start a colony there in 986.

AD 1000 The Vikings start a small settlement at L'Anse Meadows, Newfoundland.

First use of a compass in China. It will not be used in Europe for hundreds of years.

1096 The Crusades begin. Crusaders travel from Europe to the Middle East to spread Christianity. Crusades continue periodically for almost two hundred years.

1250 The Silk Road opens between Europe and China. It is in use for about one hundred years. New products and ideas are spread.

1271 Marco Polo travels to China and stays for twenty-four years. He returns to Italy in 1295.

1332 Bubonic plague originates in India. It arrives in Europe in 1347. Between 1348 and 1350, about seventy-five million people die of the Black Death.

1350 The Aztec Empire is established in Mexico and lasts until 1519.

1405 Chinese expeditions in the China Sea and Indian Ocean until 1433. Chinese ships reach Africa in 1417. After this brief period, the Chinese withdraw from further sea exploration.

1415 The Portuguese begin exploration of the African coast.

1436 The European Age of Discovery begins when Prince Henry the Navigator encourages expansion of Portuguese voyages of exploration.

1438 The Inca Empire flourishes in Peru until 1532.

1455 First use of printing in Europe. Better and more widespread communication becomes possible.

Trade begins between Africa and Portugal. First African spices and goods reach Europe. African slaves brought to Portugal.

1488 Bartolomeu Dias reaches the tip of Africa and rounds the Cape of Good Hope, in the Portuguese search for a sea route to the East Indies.

1492 Columbus sails from Spain on August 3. Arrives in the Bahamas on October 12. Sails to Cuba and Haiti.

1493 Columbus begins his second journey on September 25. He sails to Puerto Rico, Dominica, and Jamaica.

1494 Portugal and Spain sign the Treaty of Tordesillas, dividing the undiscovered world between them.

1497 John and Sebastian Cabot voyage to North America for England and reach the east coast of Canada. In 1498, John Cabot disappears on his second journey to North America.

1498 Columbus, on his third journey, discovers the Orinoco River and sails along part of the coast of South America.

1498 Vasco da Gama reaches India after sailing around the tip of Africa. Portugal now has a sea route to the East Indies.

1499 Amerigo Vespucci sails from Spain to South America. Sailing for Portugal in 1501, he ventures farther south along the coast.

1500 Pedro Alvares Cabral discovers Brazil and claims it for Portugal.

1502 Columbus sails on his fourth and final voyage, to Central and South America.

1509 Beginning of the slave trade in the New World. Spaniards take Africans by force to the Americas.

1513 Vasco Núñez de Balboa crosses the isthmus of Panama and sights the Pacific Ocean.

1514 Smallpox, brought by the Spaniards, begins to decimate the native population in Mexico and South America.

1519 Ferdinand Magellan departs from Spain on September 20 to sail around the world with a crew of 230 to 250 men.

1522 Magellan's ship, the *Victoria*, returns to Spain after successfully circumnavigating the globe. The voyage took almost exactly three years to complete.

1538 On Mercator maps, the name America is first used and the New World is divided into North and South America.

1585 English colonization begins in North America. This will eventually lead to the establishment of thirteen colonies along the east coast of North America.

SOME PEOPLE OF THE ANCIENT AND EARLY AMERICAS

The Olmecs lived on the gulf coast of Central America from about 1200 BC to about AD 300. They were the first complex society in the Americas. They expanded inland to Mexico, building cities, temples, and huge stone sculpture. They started the calendar and language upon which the Maya later built their systems.

The Maya lived in Mexico and Central America from about 1500 BC to about AD 1526. They studied astronomy and mathematics and devised an accurate calendar. They built huge cities, with temples, pyramids, palaces, ball courts, and observatories. Their system of writing (AD 100) was the only complete written language in Pre-Columbian America.

The Adena, the **Hopewell**, and the **Mississippian** peoples, all mound builders, lived in North America from about 700 BC to about AD 1500. They built enormous earthen mounds at hundreds of sites from the Ohio Valley to Texas and Florida. These geometric earthworks often contained elaborate burial and ceremonial centers.

The Zapotecs lived in southern Mexico from about 400 BC to about AD 850. They had what is probably the earliest known system of writing in the Americas and were the first to record their history. Monte Alban was their huge political and ceremonial center.

The Nazca lived in southern coastal Peru from about AD 100 to 600. They created large-scale line drawings depicting animals, flowers, and shapes. These earthworks stretch for miles and can best be seen from above.

The Anasazi lived in the desert southwest of North America. They constructed gigantic pueblos, including Pueblo Bonito in Chaco Canyon, which had 800 rooms. They lived in this area from about AD 300 to 1300.

The Toltecs lived in Mexico from about AD 900 to 1200. They were a militaristic society, and they captured many Mayan cities. They created massive stone sculpture.

The Mixtecs lived in southern Mexico from about AD 900 to 1100. They defeated the Zapotecs and took over their mountain locations. They created intricate mosaics and jewelry using colored stones and gold. Their codices (books) made of deerskin or bark were filled with colorful and detailed pictures.

The Chimu lived in northern coastal Peru from about AD 1000 to 1470. They built the city of Chan-Chan, the largest and most populous city in Pre-Columbian America. They mined gold and silver and had an advanced system of irrigation. They were overpowered by the Inca.

The Aztecs lived in Mexico from about 1350 to 1519, when they were overpowered by the Spaniards. They worshipped the Sun God and practiced human sacrifice (as did many other Pre-Columbian societies) which they considered essential to their survival. They built canals and had large trade networks.

The Inca lived in Peru from about 1438 to 1532, when their empire was destroyed by the Spaniards. The Inca, noble people of high birth, ruled over a society of thirty-two million. They built a system of highways that included thousands of miles of paved roads, bridges, and tunnels.

THE AGE OF DISCOVERY

Once European trade with the Far East began, many countries became interested in finding better and faster routes to that region. The search for a sea route to the Far East ultimately led to the discovery of the New World. The Portuguese were leaders in the effort to sail around Africa and across the Indian Ocean. They began these explorations around 1415 and soon discovered a number of islands in the Atlantic, near Portugal and north Africa, and then began to sail down the African coast.

Prince Henry the Navigator founded a naval institute in Portugal around 1436 as a training school for sailors. Sailors in both Spain and Portugal were trying to develop a better sailing ship for the long voyages they wished to attempt. Around 1442, the first **caravel** was built. The caravel was more sophisticated than earlier ships. It had two or three masts and used two types of sails. It was about 65 feet long. These new vessels allowed for greater maneuverability, thereby enabling explorers to undertake longer and more difficult journeys.

Two other events in Europe at about this time aided the advancement of the Age of Discovery. The **Gütenberg Bible**, the first book to be printed by movable type, was published in Europe in 1455. That marked the beginning of the mass production of printed matter. New knowledge could now be spread both widely and quickly (at least by the standards of the day) for the first time. In 1475, the first European printing of **Ptolemy's *Guide to Geography*** led to a revival of his theories and stimulated further European exploration. By 1517, the Portuguese had reached India and China by sea and had opened factories in Africa and India.

Once the New World was discovered, competition among rival European countries, to be the first to trade with and later colonize the new lands, increased the pace of the voyages of discovery. Spain, Portugal, England, France, and, later, Holland all participated in this race with great enthusiasm.

HOW THE AMERICAS GOT THEIR NAME

When Christopher Columbus died in 1506, he still firmly believed that he had reached Asia. Amerigo Vespucci, sailing for Portugal in 1501, hoped that he would be able to achieve what Columbus had not and would finally be the one to reach the Far East by sailing west, across the Atlantic. Although Vespucci did not fulfill that dream, he made an important discovery. Using astronomical tables of the moon and planets, he was able to come up with an estimate of the circumference of the earth that was amazingly close to the actual dimensions. That led him to the conclusion that the lands that Columbus had found were actually part of a continent unknown in Europe.

When he returned to Europe, he wrote of his conclusions in a letter. His account was published as *Mundus Novus* in 1502. Because the idea of a New World was so interesting, many more articles were published about Vespucci than about Columbus. Martin Waldseemüller, a German clergyman in France, read about Vespucci and his ideas. He belonged to a small society that did some publishing of its own, and in 1507, they came out with a small volume about Vespucci. In that book, Waldseemüller suggested that the new continent be called America after Amerigo, its discoverer. A map using the new name was included. Later, Waldseemüller felt that he had made a mistake and tried to correct it. But it was too late—the name America had caught on and was being used all over Europe.

OTHER INTERESTING VOYAGES

Although many brave explorers took part in the voyages of discovery, only a few are well known to us. Because the discovery and exploration of the Americas was a long and connected chain of events, each voyage was important and had an impact on later events.

1500 Vicente Yáñez Pinzón explores Brazil and the Amazon River.

1501 Rodrigo de Bastidas explores the coast of Panama and Columbia.

1513 Juan Ponce de León first explores Florida.

1515 Juan Díaz de Solís searches for a passage to the Pacific along the South American coast.

1518 Juan de Grijalva explores the east coast of Mexico. He names it New Spain.

1519 Hernán Cortés enters Mexico. He introduces horses to the Americas.

Domenico de Piñeda explores the Gulf of Mexico.

1521 Francisco de Gordillo explores the east coast up to South Carolina.

1522 Pascuel de Andagoya leads a land expedition from Panama to Peru.

1524 Giovanni da Verrazano explores New York Bay and the Hudson River.